PREHISTORIC SHARKS

WHAT?

Sharks have been around for more than 350 million years—even 100 million years before the dinosaurs. That makes them **prehistoric**!

Modern sharks showed up during the **Jurassic period** about 150 million years ago. The most famous prehistoric shark of all is the Megalodon! The Megalodon (pronounced MEG-uh-luh-don) is said to be the largest marine **predator** to have ever lived. Its name means "giant tooth" and it's pretty obvious why. The largest recorded tooth found measures 7.48 inches (19 cm)!

7.48 INCHES (19 CM)

MEET THE MEGALODON

The Megalodon weighed an estimated 75 tons (68 tonnes) or more. The only marine animal larger is the modern day blue whale.

From the tip of the nose to the end of its tail, scientists believe the Megalodon may have grown as long as 70 feet (21.3 m) long!

Megalodon had a huge appetite! It is believed they often ate their favorite **prey**, large whales, by tearing off their fins first.

4

According to estimates, the Megalodon had a stronger bite than even the most terrifying dinosaur—the Tyrannosaurus rex!

Today, Megalodon teeth can be found all over the world. This is because they lived in every ocean.

The Megalodon's bite was 11 feet (3.4 m) wide and almost 9 feet (2.7 m) tall. That's big enough to swallow a whole school bus!

A Megalodon tooth could grow to more than 7 inches (18 cm) long. A great white shark's tooth is only 3 inches (7.6 cm)!

A MOUTH FULL OF TEETH

Sharks may have up to 3,000 teeth. They are arranged in rows. Most sharks have five rows of teeth. Sharks use their teeth to bite large chunks out of their prey, gulping down whole pieces at a time.

Megalodon had five rows of more than 270 sharp teeth that could grow as big as 7 inches (18 cm) long.

Great white sharks have 300 super-sharp triangular teeth arranged in rows (3 inches, 7.6 cm).

The Bull Shark can have up to 50 rows of teeth in its mouth!

6

A sand tiger shark's row of sharp, pointed teeth can be seen even when the mouth is closed (1 inch, 25.4 mm).

Lemon sharks have curved teeth so they can hang on to slippery fish (3/4 inch, 19 mm).

Shortfin mako sharks have long, sharp teeth that stick out of its mouth (1.16 inches, 29.5 mm).

Tiger shark teeth aren't just sharp. They have saw-like edges to cut through shells (1 inch wide by 1 inch tall, 2.5 cm by 2.5 cm).

The longnose sawshark has a long, toothy snout, as well as sharp teeth in its mouth (.3in, .76cm).

Hammerhead shark teeth are small and smooth (1/4 to 3/4 inch, 6.4 mm to 19 mm).

SHARK BITE

Sharks are constantly losing their teeth, but that's okay because new ones grow in their place!

7

TOP TEN MOST DANGEROUS SHARKS

Sharks do not normally attack humans. Most of the time, the shark thinks a person looks like its favorite food, such as a seal or sea lion. Sharks attack fewer than 100 people each year. You are more likely to be stung by a bee or get struck by lightning.

10

Hammerhead Shark (Length: Up to 20 feet or 6.1m)
Hammerheads hunt at night and take sudden and sharp turns.

9

Blacktip Shark (Length: Up to 5.2 feet or 1.6 m)
During the breeding season, more than 10,000 blacktip sharks hang out along the Florida coastline.

8

Sand Tiger Shark (Length: Up to 10.5 feet or 3.2 m)
Sand tiger sharks troll the ocean floor very close to shore.

7

Blue Shark (Length: Up to 12.5 feet or 3.8 m)
This shark is a fast swimmer with knife-like teeth.

 **6 Bronze Whaler Shark** (Length: Up to 11 feet or 3.5 m)
Also known as the copper shark, this shark often hunts in large groups.

 **5 Shortfin Mako Shark** (Length: Up to 10 feet or 3 m)
These sharks are **aggressive**, big, fast, and have very sharp teeth.

 **4 Oceanic Whitetip Shark** (Length: Up to 9.8 feet or 3 m)
The oceanic whitetip is a quick, bold, and aggressive hunter. It has been known to attack shipwreck survivors.

 **3 Tiger Shark** (Length: Up to 14 feet or 4.2 m)
Tiger sharks will eat almost anything!

 **2 Bull Shark** (Length: Up to 11 feet or 3.5 m)
Some scientists believe that some shark bites said to be from great whites are actually from bull sharks.

 **1 Great White Shark** (Length: Up to 20 feet or 6.1 m)
Unfortunately for surfers, great whites are curious and like to "taste test" objects that look interesting.

HAMMERHEAD SHARK

Latin name: *Sphyrna*
(Say it like this: suh-FEAR-nuh)

hammerhead sharks use their heads to trap their favorite meal, stingrays, on the ocean floor.

Usually, hammerheads like to be alone, but some can be found in schools of 100 or more.

Female hammerheads can give birth to up to 50 **PUPS** at one time.

SHARK BITE

There are nine different kinds of hammerhead sharks:

- winghead
- scalloped bonnethead
- whitefin hammerhead
- scalloped hammerhead
- scoophead

- great hammerhead
- bonnethead
- smalleye hammerhead
- smooth hammerhead

SHARK FAST FACTS

Length: up to 13 feet (4 m)

Weight: up to 500 pounds (226.8 kg)

Food: stingrays, bony fish, crabs, squid, lobster, and other sea creatures

Swim speed: 25 mph (40 kph)

Location: oceans all over the world

BLACKTIP SHARK

Latin name: *Carcharhinus limbatus*
(Say it like this: kar-KAR-eye-nuss lim-BAT-uss)

Blacktip sharks sometimes hunt by leaping out of the water and splashing down on their backs.

Blacktips get their name from their black-tipped fins.

Blacktips can quickly adjust their eyes in low light.

SHARK FAST FACTS
Length: up to 8 feet (2.4 m)
Weight: up to 220 pounds (100 kg)
Food: fish, skates, stingrays, squid, and **crustaceans**
Swim speed: 14 mph (22.5 kph)
Location: warm **coastal** waters around the world

SHARK BITE

Blacktip sharks live in the waters around river mouths, muddy bays, and mangrove swamps, but they do not go into **fresh water**.

13

SAND TIGER SHARK

Latin name: *Carcharias taurus*
(Say it like this: kar-KAR-ee-uss TAR-uss)

Sand tiger sharks can come to the surface to gulp air to help them float and watch for prey without moving in the water.

Sand tiger sharks always look as if they are staring because they do not have eyelids.

To clean their eyes, they roll them back in their sockets.

Sand tiger sharks can pump water over their **gills** so they can rest on the ocean bottom, unlike some other sharks that have to keep moving in order to breathe, even when they sleep.

SHARK FAST FACTS

Length: 6.5 feet to 10 feet (2 m to 3 m)
Weight: up to 350 pounds (159 kg)
Food: herring, snappers, eels, mackerels, other fish, and sometimes other sharks
Swim speed: 12 mph (19 kph)
Location: warm waters close to shore

BLUE SHARK

Latin name: *Prionace glauca*
(Say it like this: pri-on-ah-see gla-KAH)

These fast-swimming sharks are found in open water far from shore.

Blue sharks **migrate** long distances in search of food.

Most sharks live alone. Blue sharks live in large all-male or all-female schools. Scientists do not know why they do this.

Blue sharks are found more widely around the world than any other shark species.

SHARK FAST FACTS

Length: up to 12.5 feet (3.8 m)
Weight: up to 450 pounds (204 kg)
Food: almost anything, but they prefer squid
Swim speed: average 22 mph (35 kph); bursts up to 60 mph (96.6 kph)
Location: open water worldwide

The blue shark gets its name from the beautiful blue color on its back.

BRONZE WHALER SHARK

Latin name: *Carcharhinus brachyurus*
(Say it like this: kar-KAR-eye-nuss BRACH-ee-ur-uss)

Bronze whaler sharks have a highly recognizable ridge right between the dorsal fins that is bronze in color.

Bronze whalers migrate every spring and fall, traveling up to 820 miles (1,320 km).

These sharks have narrow, hook-shaped teeth.

Bronze whalers hunt in large groups.

In June or July, female bronze whalers give birth to up to 24 shark pups.

SHARK FAST FACTS

Length: 11 feet (3.35 m)
Weight: up to 672 pounds (305 kg)
Food: fish, octopi, smaller sharks, and rays
Swim speed: fast; exact speed unknown
Location: **temperate** waters around the world

SHARK BITE

The bronze whaler can be very bold when food is around.

SHORTFIN MAKO SHARK

Latin name: *Isurus oxyrinchus*

(Say it like this: iss-URR-uss ox-ih-RINK-uss)

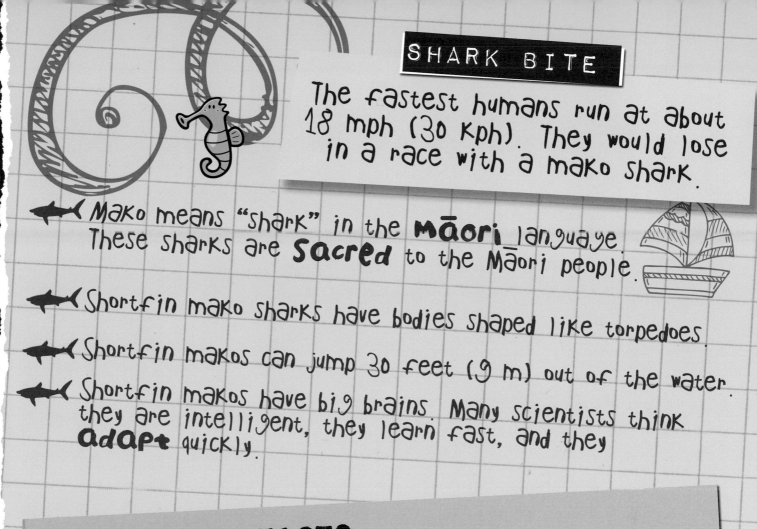

The fastest humans run at about 18 mph (30 kph). They would lose in a race with a mako shark.

Mako means "shark" in the **Māori** language. These sharks are **sacred** to the Māori people.

Shortfin mako sharks have bodies shaped like torpedoes.

Shortfin makos can jump 30 feet (9 m) out of the water.

Shortfin makos have big brains. Many scientists think they are intelligent, they learn fast, and they **adapt** quickly.

SHARK FAST FACTS

Length: 10 feet to 14 feet (3 m to 4.2 m)
Weight: up to 2,000 pounds (907 kg)
Food: fish, sea turtles, seals, and other sharks
Swim speed: average 22 mph (35 kph) with bursts up to 50 mph (80 kph)
Location: all over the world, but mostly in the western Atlantic

21

#4 OCEANIC WHITETIP SHARK

Latin name: *Carcharhinus longimanus*
(Say it like this: kar-KAR-eye-nuss LON-jem-EE-nuss)

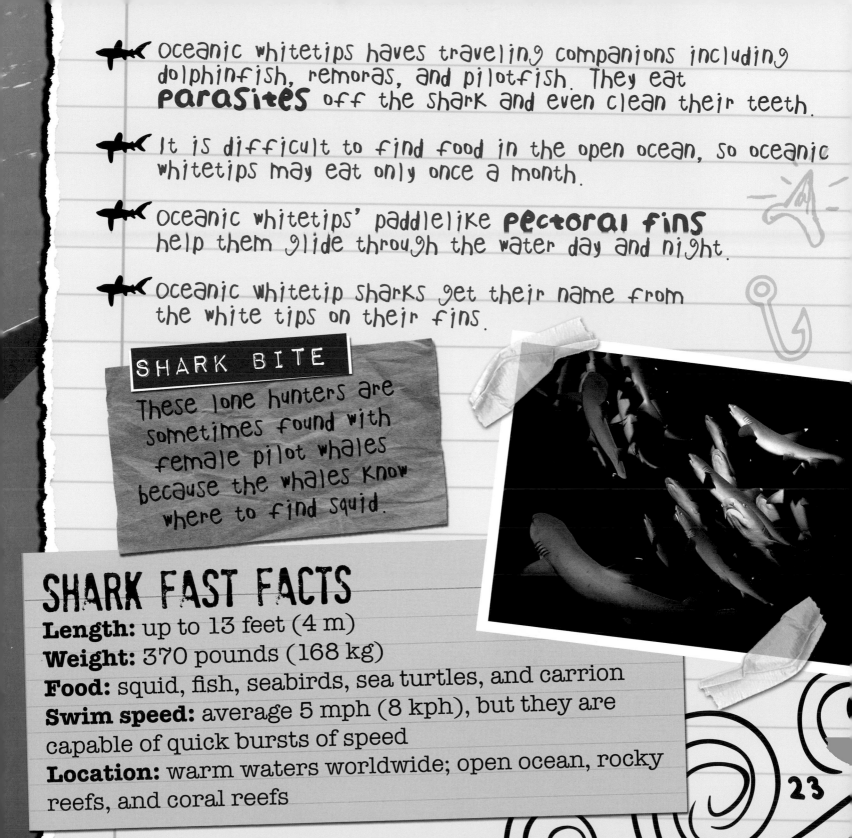

- Oceanic whitetips haves traveling companions including dolphinfish, remoras, and pilotfish. They eat **PARASITES** off the shark and even clean their teeth.

- It is difficult to find food in the open ocean, so oceanic whitetips may eat only once a month.

- Oceanic whitetips' paddlelike **PECTORAL FINS** help them glide through the water day and night.

- Oceanic whitetip sharks get their name from the white tips on their fins.

SHARK BITE

These lone hunters are sometimes found with female pilot whales because the whales know where to find squid.

SHARK FAST FACTS

Length: up to 13 feet (4 m)
Weight: 370 pounds (168 kg)
Food: squid, fish, seabirds, sea turtles, and carrion
Swim speed: average 5 mph (8 kph), but they are capable of quick bursts of speed
Location: warm waters worldwide; open ocean, rocky reefs, and coral reefs

TIGER SHARK

Latin name: *Galeocerdo cuvier*
(Say it like this: GAY-lee-oh-SER-do COOV-yay)

- Tiger sharks are known as the "garbage cans of the sea." They will eat anything!

- Female tiger sharks are bigger than male tiger sharks.

- When tiger sharks find prey, they move slowly, stalking it.

- Tiger sharks are the only kind of sharks that create eggs <u>and</u> then gives birth to live young.

SHARK FAST FACTS

Length: 10 feet to 14 feet (3 m to 4.3 m)
Weight: up to 1,400 pounds (635 kg)
Food: stingrays, sea turtles, clams, sea snakes, seals, birds, and squid
Swim speed: 20 mph (32 kph)
Location: **tropical** and **subtropical** water all over the world

#2 BULL SHARK

Latin name: *Carcharhinus leucas*
(Say it like this: kar-KAR-eye-nuss LOO-kass)

26

- Bull sharks hunt both during the day and at night.

- They will eat almost anything.

- Bull sharks are one of the few sharks that can live and hunt in **salt water** and fresh water.

- Sometimes bull sharks hunt in groups.

SHARK FAST FACTS

Length: 7 feet to 11.5 feet (2.1 m to 3.5 m)
Weight: up to 500 pounds (227 kg)
Food: fish, small sharks, turtles, birds, and dolphins
Swim speed: 25 mph (40 kph)
Location: all over the world near the shoreline

SHARK BITE

A bull shark has the strongest bite of any shark.

27

Latin name: *Carcharodon carcharias*
(Say it like this: kar-KAR-uh-don kar-KAR-ee-us)

Great white sharks can smell one drop of blood in 25 gallons (96.9 L) of water and can sense even a tiny amount of blood up to 3 miles (5 km) away.

They have torpedo-shaped bodies that help them swim fast.

Great whites are blue gray on top. Their bellies are white. This makes it difficult to see them from above and below.

SHARK FAST FACTS

Length: 15 feet to 20 feet (4.6 m to 6 m)
Weight: 5,000 pounds (2,268 kg) or more
Food: fish, seals, sea lions, small whales, and sea turtles
Swim speed: 15 mph (24 kph)
Location: cool, coastal waters around the world

SHARK BITE

Great white sharks are almost the size of a school bus.

GOBLIN SHARK

Latin name: Mitsukurina owstoni
(Say it like this: mitz-UH-kerr-EE-nuh oh-STONE-ee)

30

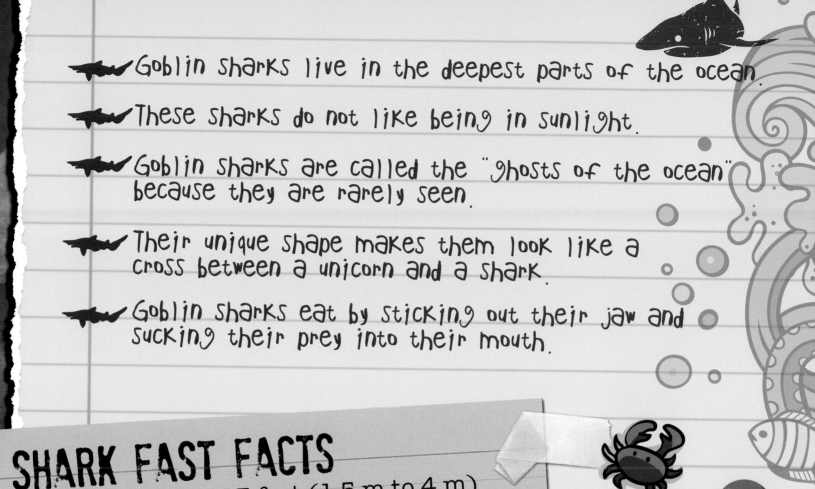

- Goblin sharks live in the deepest parts of the ocean.

- These sharks do not like being in sunlight.

- Goblin sharks are called the "ghosts of the ocean" because they are rarely seen.

- Their unique shape makes them look like a cross between a unicorn and a shark.

- Goblin sharks eat by sticking out their jaw and sucking their prey into their mouth.

SHARK FAST FACTS

Length: 5 feet to 13 feet (1.5 m to 4 m)
Weight: up to 460 pounds (208.7 kg)
Food: stingrays, mollusks, squid, and crabs
Swim speed: unknown
Location: off the coast of Japan, Gulf of Mexico, Pacific Ocean, and Atlantic Ocean

SHARK BITE

Goblin sharks are bubblegum pink in color.

GUM

MEGAMOUTH SHARK

Latin name: *Megachasma pelagios*
(Say it like this: meg-uh-KAZ-muh puh-LA-jee-ohs)

- Scientists found the first megamouth shark in 1976. Since then, there have only been 63 sightings.

- The megamouth is a giant shark that has a mouth like a **filter**, eating mostly shrimp and **plankton**.

- The megamouth shark swims in deep waters with its mouth open, but it does **breach** the surface at night.

- Megamouth sharks have up to 50 rows of teeth in their upper jaw and up to 75 rows of teeth in their lower jaw.

SHARK FAST FACTS

Length: up to 18 feet (5.5 m)
Weight: up to 2,679 pounds (1,215 kg)
Food: shrimp, plankton, small fish, and jellyfish
Swim speed: slow
Location: worldwide but in small patches of ocean

SHARK BITE

The megamouth shark is not a big danger because it has a weak body and swims poorly.

33

BLIND SHARK

Latin name: *Brachaelurus waddi*
(Say it like this: BRACK-uh-loo-rus WA-dee)

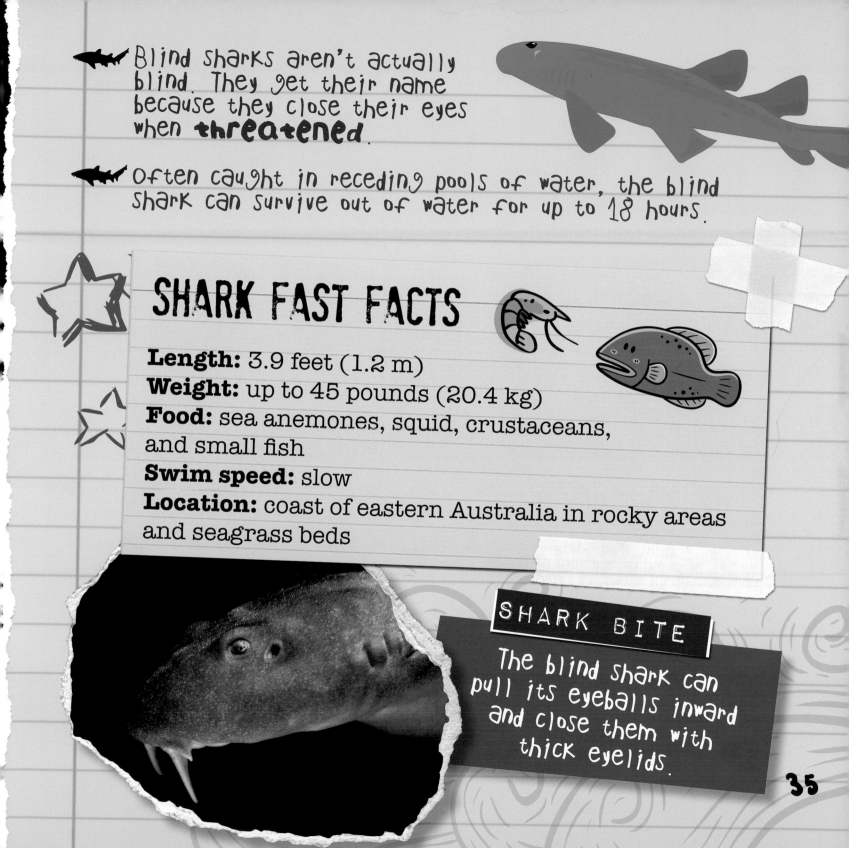

Blind sharks aren't actually blind. They get their name because they close their eyes when **threatened**.

Often caught in receding pools of water, the blind shark can survive out of water for up to 18 hours.

SHARK FAST FACTS

Length: 3.9 feet (1.2 m)
Weight: up to 45 pounds (20.4 kg)
Food: sea anemones, squid, crustaceans, and small fish
Swim speed: slow
Location: coast of eastern Australia in rocky areas and seagrass beds

SHARK BITE

The blind shark can pull its eyeballs inward and close them with thick eyelids.

FRILLED SHARK

Latin name: *Chlamydoselachus anguineus*
(Say it like this: clam-IH-duss-el-a-kuss an-GWEE-new-uss)

- Frilled sharks have lizard-like heads, ruffled throats, and long, snake-like bodies with tiny fins.

- Frilled sharks have 300 **trident**-shaped teeth arranged in about 25 rows.

- They live deep in the ocean from 165 feet to 4,200 feet (50 m to 1,280 m).

- Frilled sharks swim with their mouths open.

- They are **primitive** sharks.

Its name comes from its six pairs of frilly gills.

SHARK FAST FACTS
Length: up to 6.5 feet (2 m)
Weight: about 550 pounds (249.5 kg)
Food: mostly squid
Swim speed: very slow
Location: all over the world, but only in small spots

SHARK BITE

Scientists think the frilled shark strikes at its prey like a snake.

frilled shark teeth

ANGEL SHARK

Latin name: *Squatina squatina*
(Say it like this: skwa-TEEN-uh skwa-TEEN-uh)

Angel sharks have flattened bodies and broad pectoral fins, or "wings," that make them look like a stingray.

Angel sharks are not fast swimmers so they ambush their prey by hiding on the sea floor.

Angel sharks can strike their prey in one-tenth of a second.

Angel sharks have **spiracles** on the top of their head that pumps water through the gills while they're hiding in the sand.

SHARK FAST FACTS
Length: 4.9 feet (1.5 m)
Weight: up to 77 pounds (34 kg)
Food: fish, crustaceans, clams, and mussels
Swim speed: 2.5 mph (4 kph)
Location: shallow coastal waters throughout the world

SHARK BITE

The angel shark's nickname is "sand devil" because it hides on the sea floor and strikes with needle-like teeth.

CALIFORNIA HORN SHARK

Latin name: *Heterodontus francisci*
(Say it like this: he-TERR-oh-don-tus fran-CHISS-kee)

- The California horn shark has a small mouth full of small jagged teeth.

- The California horn shark has two fins up front that it uses to crawl over rocks in shallow water.

- The egg of a California horn shark is a leathery, corkscrew shape that the female wedges into a safe space.

- This shark has two stinging spines on its back.

SHARK BITE

This shark is also known as the walking crab cruncher.

SHARK FAST FACTS

Length: 4 feet (122 cm)
Weight: up to 60 pounds (27 kg)
Food: snails, crabs, sea urchins, and small fish
Swim speed: clumsy swimmer at 2.25 mph (3.6 kph)
Location: coastal waters worldwide

TASSELLED WOBBEGONG SHARK

Latin name: *Eucrossorhinus dasypogon*
(Say it like this: yoo-KRO-sor-ih-nus doss-ee-PO-gon)

The tasselled wobbegong shark has one of the best **camouflages** in the sea. Its tassels look like seaweed!

Even though it swims slowly, the tasselled wobbegong can catch prey in a split second.

The tasselled wobbegong will also wiggle its tassels to passing fish as bait to lure them close enough to strike.

SHARK BITE

The tasselled wobbegong has been known to attack humans when disturbed.

SHARK FAST FACTS

Length: 4.2 feet (1.3 m)
Weight: 154 pounds (70 kg)
Food: fish and invertebrates
Swim speed: slow, mostly sits on the ocean floor
Location: coral reefs in Asia, New Guinea, and Australia

43

CROCODILE SHARK

Latin name: *Pseudocarcharias kamoharai*
(Say it like this: SOO-doh-kar-KAR-ee-us KAM-o-huh-rye)

- Crocodile sharks have really large eyes that help them hunt in darkness.

- When a crocodile shark has pups, the stronger ones may eat the weaker ones while they're still in their mother's womb.

- When taken out of the water, the crocodile shark will snap its sharp teeth violently.

- The crocodile shark has an oily liver that helps it float.

SHARK FAST FACTS

Length: 3.9 feet (1.2 m)
Weight: Unknown
Food: fish, squid, and shrimps
Swim speed: Swift moving
Location: deep tropical waters worldwide

SHARK BITE

"Crocodile shark" comes from its Japanese name mizuwani, meaning "water crocodile."

LONGNOSE SAWSHARK

Latin name: *Pristiophorus cirratus*
(Say it like this: PRISS-tee-oh-for-us seer-UH-tus)

The snout of the longnose sawshark has 19 to 21 large teeth on the sides and two "feelers" called sensory **barbels**.

The "saw" of the longnose sawshark is a really long snout.

The longnose sawshark disrupts prey hiding in the sand, swiping its snout side to side.

SHARK FAST FACTS

Length: 4.9 feet (1.5 m)
Weight: up to 18.7 pounds (8.1 kg)
Food: small fish, squid, shrimp, and crustaceans
Swim speed: moderate, bottom dweller
Location: shallow coastal waters in Australia

SHARK BITE

The sensory barbels on its snout help it taste the prey hiding on the ocean floor.

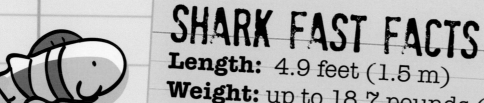

47

GLOSSARY

Adapt — to change behavior so it is easier to live in a particular place

Aggressive — mean and unfriendly in one's actions; very bold and forceful

Barbel — a thin, whisker-like sensory organ on the heads of some fish

Breach — rise or break through the surface of the water

Camouflage — using colors, materials, or light to disguise oneself as protection

Carnivore — an animal that eats the flesh of other animals

Cartilage — a tough, fibrous substance that is not as stiff as bone

Coastal — near the edge of land

Crustacean — an animal with a hard, jointed shell

Filter — to separate out

Fresh water — naturally occurring body of water that is not salty

Gills — the organs used for breathing by fish and other animals that live in the water

Jurassic period — a time in Earth's history 210 million years ago

Māori — native people of New Zealand

Migrate — to move from one place to another